21st
Century
Skills Library

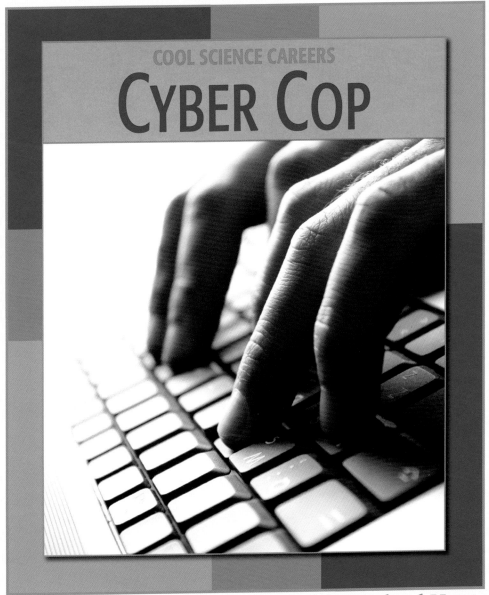

COOL SCIENCE CAREERS

CYBER COP

Patricia Freeland Hynes

Cherry Lake Publishing
Ann Arbor, Michigan

Published in the United States of America by Cherry Lake Publishing
Ann Arbor, MI
www.cherrylakepublishing.com

Library of Congress Cataloging-in-Publication Data
Hynes, Patricia Freeland.
 Cyber cop / by Patricia Freeland Hynes.
    p. cm. — (Cool science careers)
 Includes bibliographical references.
  ISBN-13: 978-1-60279-056-8 (hardcover)   978-1-60279-080-3 (pbk.)
  ISBN-10: 1-60279-056-6 (hardcover)   1-60279-080-9 (pbk.)
 1. Computer crimes—Investigation—United States—Juvenile literature. 2.
Police—United States—Juvenile literature. I. Title. II. Series.
  HV8079.C65H96 2007
  363.25'9680973—dc22   2007005624

Cherry Lake Publishing would like to acknowledge the work of
The Partnership for 21st Century Skills.
Please visit www.21stcenturyskills.org *for more information.*

TABLE of CONTENTS

CHAPTER ONE

CRIME TIME

Computer crime is a growing problem for people around the world.

Every day, our world becomes a little more dependent on computers. This can be a fine thing, but computers can also bring problems, too.

Sandra used her ATM card to pay for lunch. The card was denied, and Sandra was amazed. She was certain that she had more than $1,000 in her account. She planned to use the money to pay her college tuition and buy books. At the bank, a review of Sandra's records showed that the account had been "cleaned out" through a series of small withdrawals over the past two weeks.

Take Cory for example. He got an email he thought was from his Internet service provider.

21st Century Content

It is important to be an informed citizen. For example, by early 2006, small camera phones were so reasonably priced that many, many people bought them. Soon there were reports of these phones being used to take photos of credit cards as people used them to pay bills. For example, a thief standing behind a victim in a checkout line might lean over and photograph a card. Credit card companies and stores issued warnings and ways to foil the thieves.

It asked for his address, social security number, mother's maiden name, screen name, and password. He supplied them. A week later, he got bills—big bills—for things he never bought.

Stuart has been getting nasty emails. They are sent from several addresses, and he has received as many as 20 a day. Someone also shared his email address with several companies that sell over the Internet. Now Stuart gets ads from up to 50 of these companies every day. This SPAM, as unsolicited email is called, is going to overwhelm Stuart's computer. Any day now, if this keeps up, the computer is going to crash.

Hackers have broken into supposedly secure U.S. military computer files
as well as those of businesses, hospitals, and other organizations.

Computerized records at a big university in southern California were

invaded by a hacker. That is, an unauthorized person used computer codes

to illegally open the school's records. The school's computer personnel

found evidence of the break-in.

Whoever broke in could remove information from the school's files.

The files contained the names, social security numbers, and addresses of

Learning & Innovation Skills

Who is responsible when confidential information is taken? For example, what does the place from which the information is stolen owe to the people whose private information has been seized? Are the victims themselves responsible in any way? Debate on this issue becomes more critical as computer crimes themselves become more sophisticated. What is your opinion of this issue?

students. The files also contained information about applicants for admission, students seeking financial aid, graduates, and school employees.

Authorities at the university feared that as many as 800,000 people were affected. The university president sent letters to all these people about the possibility of **identity theft**. He urged them to carefully check credit card statements and to tell banks and credit card companies what happened, asking them to watch for suspicious activity.

Something is very wrong here.

It's time to call in the **cyber** cops!

CHAPTER TWO

WHO ARE CYBER COPS?

Many large companies, such as banks, employ large teams of cyber cops to protect their businesses and their customers.

These four stories are based on real-life happenings and describe actual cyber crimes. These are illegal acts committed using computer technology.

Cyber cops work to stamp out this type of crime. Their efforts help crime victims like those in the stories. Cyber cops also educate the public

about preventing these crimes. In the cases you just read, cyber cops were soon on the job.

Cyber cops can be members of city, county, or state police departments. They may be part of special squads within national organizations like the United States Postal Service or the Bureau of Alcohol, Tobacco, and Firearms (ATF). They may be part of the Secret Service or the Federal Bureau of Investigation (FBI). They may also work for private companies or volunteer their services in citizens' groups formed to help fight computer crime.

The work of a cyber cop can involve endless hours in front of a computer screen.

Cyber cops usually do not look for smashed windows, broken locks, and other such clues. Instead, they comb through computer files to see where and how the thieves got in. They search for weaknesses in the computer programs the victim is using. In addition, they look for cyber fingerprints—clues left behind in the computer programs that have been broken into. Through these clues, cyber cops are often able to catch the criminals and strengthen the security systems.

CHAPTER THREE

ON THE JOB

Cyber cops often specialize in a specific crime, such as theft or fraud.

In Sandra's case, the bank quickly determined that her loss was part of

a larger problem. Other bank customers had also had the money in their

accounts stolen by someone who broke into the bank's computer system.

The bank gave Sandra back the money stolen from her. Cyber cops were

put on the case. They examined the evidence that the thieves had left behind.

Cyber detectives explained to Cory that he was the victim of phishing.

In this practice, criminals send out thousands of seemingly-real emails and

All computer users need to be careful about what
kind of information they put on their computers.

Learning & Innovation Skills

SPAM is a major Internet problem. Experts and lawmakers have tried to solve the problem, but as soon as a solution is found, the criminals find a new way to send their messages. If you were a cyber cop, how would you keep up with the rapidly changing technology?

hope a few who receive them will fall for the scheme and supply personal information. Criminals use the information to get fake credit cards or buy things online.

Cyber cops advised Cory to close all his accounts and apply for new ones. They also referred him to the websites that educate people about cyber crime and how to avoid it.

Local cyber cops traced the email addresses used by Stuart's **stalker** to a classmate with a grudge, someone on the losing side in a basketball tournament. **Spamming,** or sending huge numbers of emails to a single address, turned out to be the least of this young cyber criminal's problems.

Because some of the emails contained threats, local

cyber cops contacted the FBI.

The university spent a great deal of time and

money fixing its security. At the time the problem was

discovered, it did not appear that anyone had tried to

make use of the information contained in the files.

Sometimes people who do things like this are simply

hackers. Many think that breaking into a security

system is just a sign of how smart they are. However,

in the eyes of the law, they are criminals, too.

21st Century Content

The new technologies helping law enforcement agencies around the world find cyber criminals, can be a key to 21st century learning. Scientists in the United States, Europe, and elsewhere are adapting the technologies to help young learners.

Life & Career Skills

Growing population and sophisticated technology mean we deal with more people—personally or electronically— every day. This fact makes integrity and ethical behavior a necessary character trait in personal, business, and community settings. Cyber criminals are learning that lesson the hard way.

Cyber cops have solved thousands of cases in recent years. In one, a huge ring of criminals was selling fake credit cards and personal information. The stolen information was used to withdraw money or buy things in the name of the person whose identity had been stolen. Other criminals set up a website called Darkprofits. Cyber cops from the U.S. Secret Service and the Royal Canadian Mounted Police worked with authorities in Europe to catch them.

Too often, young people are the ones committing these cyber crimes. In 2005, a teenager in western New York State was accused of spamming a popular website. He hacked into the site, got email addresses of members, and sent them more than 1.5 million advertisements. He contacted the website and offered to protect it from other criminals like himself. Cyber cops followed his electronic tracks and caught him. He faces 18 years in prison!

Too often, some people turn a wonderful new tool of 21st century life into a criminal enterprise.

CHAPTER FOUR

TRAINING

College training in economics and foreign languages would help a cyber cop solve banking crimes that originate outside the United States.

How do you fight an enemy you can't see and whose weapon—the computer—is everywhere and legal? This is where cyber cop training comes in. This training covers many academic subjects, including economics, psychology, and foreign languages. In addition, polishing up important skills and talents is part of the mix. Let's look first at the schooling.

Staying on top of the latest developments in computer science is a constant challenge for cyber cops.

A degree in computer science provides a fine basis for becoming a cyber cop. Studying international law and international relations also is good. Knowledge of languages other than English is another plus.

Learning & Innovation Skills

Just as the "bad guys" are using computers and other technologies to break the law, those innovations can be used to stop them. Think of several ways computers can be used to stop cyber criminals.

Courses in criminal justice are helpful, especially those that relate to computer crimes. In addition, each advance in the cyber world can be put to either good use or bad. Cyber cops must make sure they are ready for each new generation of "bad guys."

Being involved with computers outside the classroom is also helpful. Future cyber cops often spend time learning programming and other computer-related skills not because they have to but because they enjoy the effort.

These skills can be a great resource in fighting cyber crime. In some criminal cases, police seize the computers themselves. They can give up their secrets

The FBI, which has its headquarters in Washington, D.C., devotes a significant portion of its budget to fighting cyber crime.

to cops who know their way around a computer's innards. Cyber cops

follow the trails of the criminals through the online world, too.

More than 40 years ago, social commentator Marshall MacLuhan said

that new forms of communication such as TV had turned the world into a

Istanbul sits on both sides of a narrow waterway that separates Europe and the Middle East. Its location makes it an ideal place for criminals monitoring things in both areas.

"global village." We all know one another and what everybody else is doing.

Today this description seems even more to the point. Recently, FBI cyber cops traveled to Turkey and Morocco to share information with officials about cyber criminals operating there. This kind of cooperation can be essential to cracking a case.

In an interview, an FBI agent talked about the FBI's needs and hiring practices. The agent stressed the need for speakers of other languages and for people with highly developed computer skills. The agent said that a person with a combination of these two qualifications would be considered an ideal candidate for the FBI. Once these people have met the FBI's general hiring requirements, they would very likely be given top priority in hiring and job choice.

Some things that lead to success aren't taught. Instead, they are personal traits, abilities, and skills. One of these is the ability to communicate with

Life & Career Skills

Cyber cops need to have strong academic backgrounds. More importantly, they need to know how to keep learning. For example, the FBI's Forensic Science Research and Training Center (FSRTC) uses the newest technologies as well as time-honored thinking techniques to support FBI cases and in helping state and local law enforcement agencies.

Computer crime is often highly technical, and cyber cops must be able to clearly lay out the case to others.

people with different backgrounds and training. For example, cyber cops must be able to share complicated, technical information with lawyers on a case. The lawyers may not have much knowledge about matters dealing with the cyber part of cyber crime.

Testifying in court on cyber crimes requires very precise evidence.

Good communication skills are also important when a cyber cop testifies in court. He or she must talk to the jury in such a way that technical information is clear to them.

Gaining the trust of both coworkers and victims is necessary in all investigations. In addition, being comfortable in a variety of situations can help create goodwill. This goodwill may prove essential to a successful partnership with other agencies, both at home and abroad.

A little acting skill can't hurt either. At times the cyber cop travels through the online world pretending to be someone else. Success leads to catching potential kidnappers, stalkers, and other types of criminals.

Each organization that fights cyber crime has its own set of requirements. A candidate with most of the skills described here, however, should stand a good chance of being hired.

Pretending to be someone else when you are online is not a good idea. When professional crime fighters do this, they are targeting people already suspected of criminal activity. You should never do this kind of pretending, even "for fun." At the least, it may hurt feelings; at worst, it may get you in serious trouble.

CHAPTER FIVE

THE FUTURE

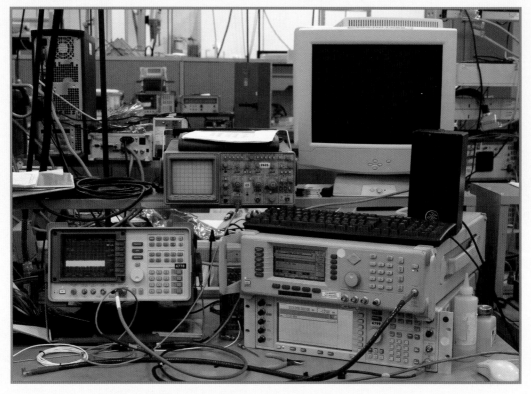

New and different computer crimes are reported every year.
Amazing and sophisticated electronic equipment helps solve them.

As computers become more sophisticated, so do cyber crimes. Many

crime-fighting organizations have formed special teams of cyber cops.

One of these types of teams is the FBI Cyber Action Teams, or CAT.

A CAT fights both present and future cyber crime.

Each team is made up of FBI agents and specialists

in computer crime. When crime threatens, a team is

ready to travel to the scene at a moment's notice.

CATs carry hardware and software that allow

them to set up a field office for up to six months

anywhere in the world. In fact, it was a CAT, together

with local authorities, that ran the successful

operations in Turkey and Morocco.

Knowing about the FBI's CAT units may be a

comfort to citizens. For the person looking into a

career as a cyber crime fighter, the organization may

be something to aspire to.

CAT is just one of several special branches within larger organizations that fight cyber crime. What might be some of the problems your CAT team would encounter working in Turkey, Morocco, or other foreign places? How might you overcome them?

GLOSSARY

cyber (SIH-bur) having to do with computer networks

hacker (HAK-er) person who breaks into important, often secret, computer files, sometimes just to see if the break-in can be accomplished

identity theft (ahy-DEN-ti-tee theft) practice of using other people's social security numbers, credit cards, passwords, and so on to buy things but charge the costs to others

phishing (FISH-eeng) plan for stealing valuable information such as credit card and social security numbers by sending email requests that appear to be from banks, credit card companies, internet service providers, and so on

stalker (STAWK-er) someone who quietly pursues another person, with no good in mind

SPAM (spam) unsolicited emails, which often appear in large amounts

spamming (SPAM-eeng) sending huge numbers of emails to a single address

FOR MORE INFORMATION

Books

Garcia, Belinda. *Alyson's Adventures in Computer Land.*
Tucson, AZ: Hats Off Books, 2005.

Hafner, Katie. *Where Wizards Stay Up Late: Origins of the Internet.*
New York: Simon & Schuster, 1998.

Leavitt, Jacalyn. *Faux Paw's Adventures in the Internet.*
New York: John Wiley & Sons, 2004.

Sherman, Josepha. *Internet Safety.* New York: Franklin Watts, 2003.

Other Media

http://www.fbi.gov/kids/k5th/safety2.htm is an FBI
website for kids about keeping safe on the Internet.

*http://www.isafe.org/imgs/pdf/newsletter/ibuddy/
ibuddy_times_fall2006.pdf* is a kid-friendly website
about Internet safety with games and activities.

INDEX

ABOUT THE AUTHOR

Patricia Freeland Hynes grew up in Pennsylvania, where she climbed hills and trees and swam in the local river. She attended college in Pennsylvania and got a degree in literature and secondary education. In both high school and college, her writing was published in school literary journals. She has spent her adult life teaching and writing for young people and has lived in Baltimore, Boston, Chicago, Florida, and Canada. She now lives in Venice, California, with her husband, a painter and dentist, and a fluffy orange cat named Stinky.